THE BUILT MOMENT

LAVINIA GREENLAW

The Built Moment

FABER & FABER

First published in 2019
by Faber & Faber Ltd
Bloomsbury House
74–77 Great Russell Street
London WC1B 3DA

Typeset by Hamish Ironside
Printed in the UK by TJ International Ltd, Padstow, Cornwall

A CIP record for this book is available from the British Library

ISBN 978-0-571-34710-0

2 4 6 8 10 9 7 5 3 1

THE BUILT MOMENT

Acknowledgements

The Guardian, London Review of Books, BBC Radio 4, Film and Video Umbrella, the Wapping Project.

The Sea is an Edge and an Ending is the title of a short film based on the sequence of the same name (see www.fvu. co.uk/projects/the-sea-is-an-edge-and-an-ending-1).

'It was me waiting for me' first appeared in *Joy Division*, a collaboration with Michael Bracewell and Glenn Brown (Enitharmon Editions, 2017).

'A difficulty with words' was inspired by conversations with Mark Wallinger about his series 'id'.

'Men I have heard in the night' was originally part of an immersive sound installation, *Audio Obscura*, commissioned by Artangel, which can be listened to at www.artangel.org. uk/project/audio-obscura.

I would also like to thank the Wellcome Trust for the Engagement Fellowship during which I completed some of this work.

Thank you to all at Faber, especially Lavinia Singer and my editor, Matthew Hollis.

Contents

THE SEA IS AN EDGE AND AN ENDING

The sea is an edge and an ending

My father has lost his way out of the present.
Something is stopping him leaving, nothing becomes
the immediate past.

The act of forgetting used to take time.
Now it accompanies him through each day
and the world folds itself up behind his every step.

What unlocked this emptiness?
He knows not to ask. He knows now how small he is,
how small his island, how small his spell.

There, he says

His wife has died, he is alone
and so we follow him into the storm
because he wants to take us out. Out where?
There, he says, as we turn each black corner, *there*.

A man in grief walking the empty centre
of a Sunday-night small town
caught up in the act of knowing where he's going
as we repeat the drenched streets.

He already has us running in circles
as if we can hold his world in place
even form a new edge.
We say to each other all he needs is rest.

His gifts

As if about to attempt an extraordinary feat
– flight perhaps –
my father is freeing himself of any obligation to the past.

And so he keeps arriving
in loose parcels he wraps as a gift:
broken books, the wisdom of his ancestors,
my mother's likeness, inscrutable souvenirs,
heirlooms he never wanted or couldn't sell.

Here, he says, *I chose this for you.*
Is this the easiest way to let go?
Not to do it yourself but to pass the act on?

My father appears

He has long been under his own spell.
Years ago he drew a circle that so enchanted me
I never thought to enter it. We rarely met.

Now and then he appeared
with a bunch of tired flowers
wanting to talk of his enemies and how he'd been cast out.

His stories led only back to their beginnings
like the last letter he sent me
in which the second page repeats the first.

My father's weakness

Whenever we have gathered round a table like this
he has been talking or drawing the talk towards himself
but now he sits among conversation
his eyes following the noise
as if we were animals grappling for meat
and he weakened, working hard to go unnoticed
to be allowed to remain.

My father on paper

He has many suspicions and locks his papers away.
Till one day he sees only paper.

He can read the details of himself no longer and so
    lays them out.
There has been so much to contain.

He lays it all out and invites me in. At last I'm in.
I read his accounts, his confessions, his treatments,

his wishes and his pain. Now I know everything
and I can't find him.

He scares me

He is doing things that are just frightening enough.
The front door left wide, a frying pan on the stove,
the heating turned off on an icy day.

He is saying: *I am unclosed, I am going up in smoke,*
   I am freezing over.
I tell him I am saving him as quickly as I can.

What my father knows

The present tense is a failed invention.
All that investment, design and loss.

My father knows to put on his coat but not to go out.
Food is to be set on the table. The kettle is to be filled.

He contemplates a pencil. A sock.
In the bathroom, he holds a towel and stands there.

What is this glorious fall of water?
What is to be done here?

My father cannot stop

When his mind perceives itself failing
like an engine questioning its parts, everything stops
and he sees what it will be like when everything stops.

The problem is that nothing stops.
Time does not remain
and terror prompts him to do what he can to be stopped.

And so he keeps setting out – without keys or money
    or a plan –
casting himself upon the world, sure that it will come:
the divine hand that reaches down to switch off
    the engine
– the point of arrest, the rest.

His diagnosis

The film my father sat down to watch on a Saturday afternoon in 1943 grew out of a scene cut from another film –
a conversation about the young not knowing what it's
like to grow old. My father was ten and hadn't begun to
conceive of himself as a being on a journey of breakdown,
revelation and decay. He knew something of life and something of death. His pockets were loaded with shell casings
and, like his friends, he could identify a fighter jet from the
shadow of a wing. He was confused by the film which started near the end and then moved through a series of battles
and romances. Was she the same woman? Wasn't that
man already old? A courier on horseback arrived and his
message flashed up: THE ITALIANS HAVE SURRENDERED.
The Italians? My father was young enough to sit in the dark
and accept whatever came along. Only when he emerged
into bright afternoon and heard someone shouting the news
did he understand that the message had been cut from
another film – the one he lived in. He too would be haunted
by women and lose houses and stand at the side of the
road while life marched past and the world retracted into
battles, romances, shadows and surrenders that are all so
small now, so far away. A message has just arrived. He tells
himself that it's part of the film and tries to leave the dark
room but this time steps out into more darkness. Doesn't
he understand? It's why someone is shouting. They have
important news.

A panorama for and of my father

Paths of chalk and water.
The perpendicular highways of night creatures.
Ridged contours and jack-knife shadows.

Cropped growth on compacted slopes.
The press from above and below.

Unreachable fields
where light is deflected, pearled and pooled
so that it just hangs there.

I have put my father in another room

He sleeps like a low flame and wakes to new laws.
His soul is allowed to wander.
His landscape is one of gentle peripheries.
His world weighs no more than he can hold
and consists of what he has in view: on fair days a garden
where kind women come to collect him.

I do not want to open the door.
The old will meet me there, my father among them.
They'll show me that it is before we die
that we become some other thing
– stone, a cloud perhaps, a tree of knots.

His home comes apart at the touch

He has never felt as present
as he does now that the place is empty.

It's as if what's most determined in him
has decided to remain

abandoning the man who has entered a contract
with corridors and menus, footstools and
    emergency cords.

I have opened every drawer, removed each lid
and reached into every pocket and yet I
    – his daughter –

am still not sure what he means.
Roman coins. Elastic bands. A pencil with a tassel.

My father remembers

One by one he is raising the decades of his life
    up out of himself.
It's as if he's built in himself a small crane
– the kind used in a cargo hold for minor acts
    of rearrangement.

Only the hold has flooded, the cargo's afloat
and the crane's hook swings to and fro
grabbing whatever is bumped within reach.

If I cannot find him then he must be lost

On the first of December, the cherry tree switches itself on.
The one thing lighting itself at this time.
I do not want to be lit but I need to know that those I love
are there like lights to be switched on.

I'm late for my father and rush towards him
because he has been returned to me and now is my chance
    to love him.
When I arrive he doesn't know I'm late or that I was
    on my way.
When I leave he will not know that I have been.

He is already there. In a land that lacks dimension.
The sea spreads itself between us.
Storm follows storm. Why not admit this?
The late soft colours of his returning to me are already gone.

My father rises whenever

He runs a bath at four a.m.
and wanders into neighbours' rooms.

Nothing tells him not to open doors or that it is dark.
Is it never dark for him now?

The last time he could tell me what he did all day
   he said
I run things in my head.

I lie awake at four a.m. and think about his head.
The bombed streets and brute structures.

Uncoupled engines
shunting themselves up and down brief tracks.

My father tells me to wait

When I arrive he is eating and I'm told to wait,
to let him finish, not to unsettle him. I wait.

When he finally sees me
it's as if he's been brought to an open door

and made to peer into a dark night.
He's afraid to ask who's there. *What if someone's there?*

He'd have to invite them in and accompany them
    through time.
He peers at me and the space between us extends itself

so that I am where he wants me, out there in the dark
in a place without stars or fathers

and he raises his hand and says *Stay there, stay there.*

My father has no shadow

Suddenly he has one mood and it is sweetness.
Is this the unshadowed self he once was
before the loss and pain that came to him so young?
Are such shadows what give us form?
Has he abandoned loss and pain?
Is that why I cannot see him?

His freedom

He blesses the sound of pigeons and children
and loves us all.
He knows that he can still cure anything.

I thought I was guarding him from a crowded darkness
but now he stands free, locked into brightness.
His world is wonderful.

While he can still speak

He tells his hands to put on his shoes
and encourages his legs when getting dressed.
He has become his own messenger
carrying orders for what once simply occurred.
This works as long as he can put them into words.

My father's loss of feeling

I'd been talking about feeling and how we want to feel
but what we hope for from feeling is total and opaque
which is what we hope for from not feeling too.

And how feeling and not feeling are one desire
– for enlargement out of the self –
and the loss of detail and qualification this brings.

So my father who has lost detail and qualification
should feel without discrimination.
He should feel everything as if it were nothing and he does.

The finishing line

If I weren't here, my brother said on the third of the four days we sat by our father, I'd be running a race dressed as a gorilla. I thought it'd be alright because there'd be four of us, colleagues, all dressed as gorillas. Then last week the suits arrived and we tried them on and someone said we needed to practise running while dressed as gorillas. We were standing there in the office, wearing the suits, realising what we were about to do: run through the streets in plain view, dressed as gorillas. Someone came over to us, the four hesitant gorillas, and asked if there was a problem. What will people think, we said, if they see four gorillas running through town? Won't they wonder why? Don't worry, he said, I have an idea. I'll dress up as a banana and run ahead and you can chase me. And this was what my brother and his colleagues did. Not feeling foolish because now they had evident purpose – and we laughed as we sat by our father, laughed at old stories too, and laughed when the nun invoked his spirit to rise and leant over him, her knee pressing the button that lifted his pillows so that he did indeed rise, and we laughed when he stopped breathing for twelve seconds and then started again, laughed out of astonishment that those four days were real and he was leaving us, stepping out of his fancy dress to no evident purpose, going nowhere with no one leading the way.

Four days, three nights

His body opens like flower after flower
and with each failure to contain
he gives up the equivalent in shame.
The maidens are permitted to immerse him.
To run a blade across his skin.
To reach into his buttons and zips.
To reach into him with gloves.
To place things in his hands and in his mouth.
To place him. To arrange him.
To stroke his throat so that he swallows.
To lift his body every four hours out of its shadow
and to place something clean and blank beneath.

My father leaving

I have found a form for my grief in the memory of
    a young deer
I glimpsed by the side of the road half destroyed half poised
to make a leap.

The snow held in place its shock
at being collapsed back into the earth while yet to know
what it was here for or what needed to be done.

Did you think the earth had taken hold
the day you pulled off the road and walked away from
    your wife
and four children as if we stopped your breath?

All we could do was line up to watch you disappear.

Do I have to stand there forever while my body gives way
as it did in the years in which you could not stop leaving?
Will you stop leaving now?

THE BLUEBELL HORIZONTAL

The bluebell horizontal

Deep woods.
Bright shallows overwhelming
a crowd of vertical tensions.

Chroma

From today the days will start building
but light will never seem as perfect a form of deletion
as it does right now
loosened into a cold sprawl

as if space has risen through image
and I am no longer travelling home but outwards
and into this.

The break

Deep in the dark of that year
I issued a warning. *I'm going to break*, I said
but quietly and so often that it sounded like a refrain.
People nodded and moved on. What else could they do?
Hold me? Through each and every day?
They had their own days.
One night something paused in the empty street
and tipped me sideways before moving on
and I discovered the pain I'd been trying to speak of.
I was two things now – the shocked engine
and the broken part I carried the last mile home
as if it were something I could then set down.
I met every kindness that followed with astonishment
even when they held up pictures and said
You have every reason to be in such pain.
They had looked inside me and found reasons.
To my mind, these people were gods.
I told my beloved I'd look after myself
but he kept approaching with care and patience
while I issued warnings as a form of encouragement.
There was an instant simplification of our long romance:
we spoke only of pillows, medication, tea and bread.
For months I woke beside my pain
and waited for it to knit itself to me – to become something
I carried without feeling, something incorporated
to the extent that it is not known.
Why, when I had the chance, did I not just set it down?
In what way does it complete me?

Where are we now?

I am a girl who looks like a boy who looks like a girl
and everything is going to be alright.

The one I will love, when I'm old enough to love,
is waiting for me out there
among the puddles and cardboard boxes
wearing emerald lurex and a gold crest.

His attributes, including his boyness,
will throw themselves into reverse
and I will learn that mine can do so too.

One of these is his voice
which begins in the murmur of loose straw
and ends in the loneliness of a mountain king.

He will demonstrate the ability to detach
himself from himself
but to remain present, side by side.

He will teach me to offer something to look at
so as not to be seen.

That in order to be heard, I must not repeat myself.
Nor must I depend on anyone listening.

He will always be leaving
even as he sings and he will sing to me long after
the door is closed.

He is gone.
Exiled to the flat fields we must dance to this.
We must perfect our routine.

Flowers for G.T.

I would have met your pain with my body
and lain with you as in the hours of our youth
with all youth's ceremony.

I would have taken you back to our first walk
at dawn across a borrowed town – wakeful, speechless
and amazed by new feeling.

I would have met you in love
instead of in what you feared of love, which I feared too.
We would not have been so young.

The day I heard of your illness and its end
white flowers in the lane were shaking out their brightness.
They could not stop shaking.

Perhaps we should have just keep walking
beyond dawn, beyond town, beyond desire and fear
and death and pain. Beyond the bright flowers shaking.

It was me waiting for me

We told the old stories of the future.
Were we living it?

Everywhere was aftershock:
the decay of an event so fundamental
it passed unremarked.

Everywhere was a small town shutting up early
while the young gathered to contemplate
violence – the one thing they could make occur.

*

The great halls were empty.
The air so chill and damp and trapped
it bloomed in slow roses.

The cinemas and stations
that had been our guardians for so long
entered a sleep from which they would wake recast
as we would wake to find ourselves in middle age.

The edge of the island was empty.
We gathered at the silent dock and waited for new
    ways to leave.

*

We danced in rooms built for the arrival
of cotton and grain by water or steam.
We met in market squares and tobacconists.
We dressed as spies and highwaymen.
All roads were open and unlit.

*

Someone was making the noise we wanted to
about feelings we didn't know we had.

We dealt in insight, relying on the one solid phrase.
We wrote, and spoke, in capital letters.

We wanted scale and depth and glamour
and found them in disused space and a failure to connect.

This was our noise.

*

A boy waiting to feel
or to find someone who could show him how to

when what arrived was so total
it had neither the shape nor direction that feeling requires.

*

For all the books and methods and rules,
the medication and the blue room,
the sidesteps, variants and deletions, the different endings

he could not reach himself and met only himself
turning away.

The built moment

We gather great stones and put our years into moving them.
Do we think of them as landmarks or an extension
   of vision?
Do they prove the existence of time?
The poor humans. Vigilance to the point of magic:
a hand reaching out to catch something we have yet
   to see fall.
Let there be ground and places where ground gives shape
to where it's missing. Think of crossing a room
and finding at its centre a small but infinite ravine:
pressure finding its way through weakness
as in machines or weather or time.
Time is not place. We cannot build on it
but still we think the process good for us and seek it out.

Yellow, lichen

Two things living within one another.
One offers structure, the other the conversion of light.
Drawing on rain and dust, they create something
    beyond themselves.
Its growth is slow to the point of magnificence.
Do not mistake this colour for strength,
its warmth for noise or its shading for form.

Pyroxene

Is this how it was when they worked on your heart?

A thunderbolt above the house
that lifts me from sleep as if out of the earth
and sends my blood running in reverse?

Did they enter each chamber as if it were a cave
in which they'd glimpsed the most unexpected
architectural formations?

What of you did they have to unbuild
in order to restore the idea of a heart
as either empty or full?

And what did you keep to yourself
so that all that makes its way in
is still met with a test

– your transformation of flow into emphasis?

Slowly and from within

High summer in a seaside town
where the streets are full of families out for the day
being a family and for all I know content
and even, some, approaching joy
but my body aches for them.
Who are these people wandering, exhausted,
  in terrible grief?
It is my grief. All day it nudges
like something swimming up to be fed,
its eyes empty, its mouth not opening.

We try to accommodate our dead
and make space in ourselves which they do not enter
having their own space beside us.
Slowly and from within we must determine
to give that space its freedom
and not to keep building on loss.

A time when work was visible

When asked what we did all day we could point to
    the fire,
to the gathering steam, the pressure, the ashes.
We could make sense of movement and change.
For simple decisions there were levers.

Our machines needed us.
We listened to them and made adjustments.
We held tools and gathered material in our bare hands.
Our bodies recorded these contacts.

Then our tools became so small that we carried them
    in boxes
which we did not have to open and so did not learn how.
Our surfaces grew bland through lack of contact
and we found new pain in reducing our gestures.

Now work is air.
We spend our days imagining it.

Desynchronosis

The night train slows as it crosses a plateau of flood water
and now we are listening.

The engine held back
is finding it hard to give up the moment – a form of regret

like that of the body returning home out of time
the days of coming into land

when sleep is music
(but what instruments and how to play them?)

or sleep is the black pool
across which we steal our way.

It is the passing through and not what is so full
that we are all impatient to attend to.

Numberless falls

After any first shock
the next finds its shape waiting.

Water as cold as this
travels an edge of its own making.

Each next time adds to the ice
and narrows the flow.

The frozen cascades
of what cannot pass into feeling or be let go.

Men I have heard in the night

Please take this anger and this pain
and let me feel the love I know I have
and let me be able to speak of love and show love
and let it fall away
the terrible weight and the pain
and let me be good as I am good in my heart
and let it not hurt to remember
and let it stop and let me leave behind
all that has built itself into my heart
and let me find the words and let there be time
and let me open my heart
and let the hope be met with love
and all the wanting be simple and good
and let me be loved
and let me be allowed to be good.

Wintersweet

So slight against the black branch
its scent outweighs it
(and clouds the path
forcing me to step aside into
a long-ago far-off place of sweet winters
now blank compactions
of occasion, detail, horror and swoon:
tiny densities carried into the house
on their looming perfume).

Fleur de sel

A trace of violet on the tongue.
So delicate a recognition of true nature
as unclear and soluble and free.

Heaven is loved ones rising
out of the sun and walking with me
into the sea.

A difficulty with words

APPREHENSION

To be caught in the act – any act

GESTURE

A dream of direct contact

MOVEMENT

Simultaneous disarrangement and orchestration

IMAGE

The mind forcing the eye to conclude

FOCUS

The need to go so far that there is no coming back

EXPRESSION

The need to forget what I am doing

LANGUAGE

As a form of curiosity

RHYME

Occurring emphatically within the confines of the self

VESSEL

What I, in my symmetry, invite

CAPACITY

What I, in my symmetry, arrest

DEVELOPMENT

That I am not I

REFLECTION

I will overturn

DESCRIPTION

Resistance to experience

TONE

Resistance to atmosphere

DENSITY

Turning inwards in order to form

ARGUMENT

The insecurity of subject and object

FRAY

Trying to keep human shape

DELETION

Must remain

SELF-EXPLANATORY

As in explaining to myself

PURPOSE

To fulfil the act of making

INTENTION

Years later

A FLAW

Exemption

OVERSIGHT

Truculence in the face of meaning

DIGRESSION

An investment in what might relate

CONCENTRATION

The reader as a form of dilution

IN BLACK AND WHITE

A refusal to decide which is silence and which phrase

OUTLINE

Because the I of the poem is not the first person
but the person

I AM STILL I

Because the I must be on intimate terms with itself
in order to undress itself

UNCERTAINTY

As a form of commitment

ABSENCE

To which nothing must adjust

COMPLETION

An arrangement that can place what is not its part

ABANDONMENT

And yet –